T0355043

SANDBOX
101

Where A **Lifetime**
Of Learning Begins

JEROME B. IMHOFF

Order this book online at www.trafford.com
or email orders@trafford.com

Most Trafford titles are also available at major online book retailers.

Print information available on the last page.

ISBN: 978-1-6987-1887-3 (sc)
ISBN: 978-1-6987-1888-0 (e)

Library of Congress Control Number: 2025902248

Trafford rev. 02/19/2025

 www.trafford.com

North America & international
toll-free: 844-688-6899 (USA & Canada)
fax: 812 355 4082

DEDICATION

To my parents and grandparents. Without their guidance, time and example, writing this book would not have been possible. To the children of all ages who take the spirit of these lessons and apply them to their own lives.

ACKNOWLEDGMENTS

My thanks go out to my "old" friends, Raymond Leger, James Burke and David Colton, to my teachers and co-workers who taught me the ropes, contributed their individual and collective knowledge and experience to my life and helped me augment this book with the wisdom of the ages. To my brothers Ed and John who helped me with structure and proofreading.

Some of the lessons will be familiar to the readers, others not so much, but each has a place in the order of our lives lived to their fullest. We have shared full careers and life after those careers, and each of you has been instrumental in the creation of this book.

FORWARD

I am always saying to myself, I wish I could have known all these things when I was growing up, that I know now. I wish I could take my aging adult mind and understand those things and place them in the child that I once was. Would I have approached life differently? In some cases, of course, in others, perhaps not.

When we are children, everybody our age is at the beginning of what promises to be a long and complex journey. Along the way, we will meet, influence, interact with, and be influenced by thousands of people who will be experiencing the same journey in ways unique to them. What will my contribution to their journey be and what will be my influence on their life? The answers to those questions are both, we don't know. Much of it will depend on what we have learned along the way and how we apply that which we have learned.

Try to learn something each day and try to have a positive impact on those you encounter. It won't always be easy, but it will always be worth the effort to make a difference.

Edward F. Imhoff

CONTENTS

CHAPTER 1

SANDBOX 101

Learning begins early in life and often we don't remember the initial onset of the process. Often, we look back from adulthood and we remember or wonder where we heard that before or what was the theory that preceded the practice.

It was 1952, Hargrove Street, Madison, Wisconsin. I was only four years old and dad had just put the spring load of sand in our 8 X 8-foot back yard sandbox. There we were with the neighbor kids from the house behind ours, my brother John and me, reveling in the new sand that covered the hard packed mix of sand and dirt left over from last year.

There were four of us and there is a system involved in occupying the same controlled space. First, you had to learn to share. One kid gets the old metal dump truck with one wheel missing. One gets the pail and shovel. One gets the tin cup and saucer and one gets the scraping stick. There isn't a protocol involved. It's whoever comes first, gets the choice.

Without knowing what it was, we were learning the rudiments of communication, sharing and negotiation. Sharing can take practice. Sharing toys and tools, space and time is a lifelong pursuit. As we get older, it turns into "partnering" and we realize that sights and sounds, projects, vocations, and avocations are more satisfying and enjoyable if shared with others. It all started in the sandbox.

I remember asking my brother if he wanted to trade sandbox tools and hearing my first words of rejection, "no way!" Of course, no one wanted the scraping stick. We made hills, roads and tunnels that caved in on the metal truck with one wheel missing. I learned that throwing sand didn't accomplish anything except making my brother mad and the neighbor kids didn't want to play rough, so they went back across

1

the fence. Now it was just my brother and me and he was older, stronger, probably wiser and knew more about manipulating little brothers. At 74, I still don't like being manipulated or bullied.

When the neighbor kids left, there were more resources and less competition. At age 4, girls were still just kids, like cups without handles. They're just cups. There was less fun, fewer people to listen to and nobody with whom to establish a bond or alliance. None of that dawned on me yet, at age 4 but as time passed, each became a building block in the development of my personality. The traits experienced in the sandbox are more complex and more consequential and are still recognizable to this day.

CHAPTER 2

LISTEN TO THE OLD MEN

Normal communication is usually 50% talk and 50% listening. At other times it's just active listening. It was 1955, Atwood Avenue, Madison, Wisconsin, Hoveland's Barber Shop. Julius Hoveland, my great uncle was the proprietor and barber. On days when it was raining too hard to walk the mile and a quarter home from St. Bernard's School, I'd walk one block down the street to Uncle Julius', knowing that I was always welcome there. Uncle Julius was a big, burly kind old Norwegian with a round face and lace up high top orthopedic shoes. I'd sit in the big bay window and read comic books while he would slide into the empty barber chair and hold court with two or three other old men. They'd discuss the events of the day in Madison and beyond. Through the gravely voices and cigar smoke, I heard about how local and national politics impacted their daily lives. I heard stories about stock cars and farm tractors, movies and trains, wives, children and grandchildren and how important they all were in the grand scheme of things. They never asked for my input. I sometimes wondered if the old men in the hard oak chairs even realized I was there, but I listened as they talked and laughed, agreed and disagreed, but they never really fought. I learned that men could disagree without being disagreeable.

Now, almost 70 years later, old men still gather (not the same old men) They're mostly forest service volunteers. They gather on winter mornings sitting on stools in the shop at the top of the hill and I'm still listening. We drink coffee, share experiences, appreciate each other's company and plan the activities of the day.

It reminds me of Uncle Julius's barber shop and the old men in the hard oak chairs. History can repeat itself with a different setting and a different cast of characters. I have become one of the old men and I wouldn't have it any other way.

Some old men like to tell tall tales to young boys who are eager to listen and every once in a while, but not very often, one of those ever so slightly embellished tall tales will be true.

> Back when I was probably 10 or so, I went with my grandparents to their little house trailer on Lake Wisconsin. The little campground was run by an old man with green Dickie trousers and red suspenders named Dave Thistle. He wore rimless glasses and a beat-up pork pie hat and was a master of the tall tale. One evening, Grandpa Duckert and I were sitting on the battered bench by the boat launch with Mr. Thistle. Grandpa had forewarned me about Mr. Thistle's habit of stretching the truth, more than just a little. This was such a tale, or so I thought. Mr. Thistle told me (in confidence of course) that there was an 8 ft. sturgeon in the live tank by the bait shop. Grandpa, Mr. Whittaker from Illinois and Reverend Dirksen, from the Presbyterian church in Cottage Grove, all laughed at the story, even when Mr. Thistle protested to no avail, but I was still curious, having never seen a fish that big, but Dave was undeterred. He said, "Come on, young fella. Let's go see" and sure enough, there in the live tank, stretching from one end to the other, was an 8 ft. sturgeon. Without so much as a blink of an eye, I went back to the bench, sat down next to Grandpa Duckert, poked his arm and said (in as honest a voice as I could muster) "Mr. Thistle has an 8 ft. sturgeon, right over there in the live tank by the bait shop. Grandpa just smiled.

Every now and then, the teller of tall tales will tell you the truth, but not very often.

CHAPTER 3

RESPONSIBILITY

It's a big word that covers a lot of ground. It means something different to each person or group. Of the utmost importance, it starts with responsibility to and for YOURSELF. It means knowing right from wrong and living that knowledge day in and day out, in little things and big. It's lying or choosing to tell the truth when lying would be easier. You might get away with a lie temporarily. You might breathe a sigh of relief and say to yourself, "Whew! I got away with it and someone else got in trouble instead of me" …But… deep inside, your conscience might gnaw at you and you'll either admit what you did, or you'll get caught red handed by someone who heard, saw or knew the truth. The odds are always stacked against the liar, and the consequences of not taking responsibility for yourself and your behavior toward others, can follow you through the rest of your life.

Responsibility to and for others is on a whole different level, the older you get, the greater the responsibility. Parents are responsible for their children. Teammates are responsible to each other. Soldiers and police officers are responsible for the safety of those who work and serve with them and to the public who trust them for their safety. EMT's, doctors and nurses in hospitals are responsible for the patients under their care and presidents are responsible to govern with honesty and integrity. You will learn that that doesn't always happen, but that's for another conversation. As we age and go through life, responsibilities grow and can become more complex. Be ready for the transition. It's coming.

CHAPTER 4

BE THOUGHTFUL. BE KIND.

Look at your parents and your friends and try to find these traits in them. Then look at yourself, your choices and interactions with those around you. Are you thoughtful, or do you disregard the opportunities that pass in front of you each day? When a situation gives you a choice to be kind or to be aloof, distant or unkind, which do you choose. Are kindness and consideration part of your personality, or do you have to "fake it," or work at it begrudgingly? For some, these traits come naturally. They have watched parents, grandparents, teachers and friends who were helpful and understanding when things weren't going all that well for someone else.

Sometimes it's not easy to be kind or thoughtful. When negative things happen, you might retreat to a mindset that is more defensive. When the bully is picking on you, you can easily forget that he or they don't think the way you would like to think. They may have been raised in a home where parents weren't nice to each other or anyone else, or where an older brother was angry all the time and took it out on younger siblings, perhaps you. The negative traits come naturally, if that is all you've ever seen at home. Our early experiences teach us behavior patterns that can last a lifetime.

There is no way to insulate yourself from reality. There are good people who are inherently good and kind. People sometimes say "they were born that way." People are not born mean or unkind. Most of them learned that behavior from someone else. They get a short-term gain from picking on someone who won't or is unable to fight back. To them, it's like a victory, no matter how hollow.

It makes them feel powerful or important because they've got nothing else to fall back on to motivate them to change their behavior. Some go through their entire lives like that. Bullies can become aggressive adults without anyone being able to get emotionally close enough to show them that there is indeed a better, more productive way to conduct themselves, they may never change. Their lack of sensitivity leads to social isolation, depression and hostility. If you are put in a position to choose your behavior, choose wisely. The decision could impact your entire life.

CHAPTER 5

KEEP YOUR MIND ON THE FUTURE YOU'LL SPEND YOUR LIFE THERE (CLASS MOTTO, MONONA GROVE HIGH SCHOOL, CLASS OF 1966)

Think about that sentence and how absolutely true it is. 1966 might seem like a really long time ago but the motto is relevant still today. Your primary focus will usually be on the events of today, school, sports, friends, jobs, and what's going on here and now. Teenage life is full of distractions that keep you up late, talking to your friends after your parents have gone to bed. Being socially ready for the next challenge or adventures in the morning is important to you. ...But.......there is life after "Right Now," and it would be smart to embrace that fact in between the trials and tribulations of today. Homework not done today may add to the homework of tomorrow. Slacking off on chores for the man next door may cost you another job that is better. As you get older, the consequences of not following through on a job or a project could cost you a position on a team or a job that went to someone else. Life doesn't begin or end when you're 11 or 12 or 15. It's the beginning and work habits follow study habits and looking from one to the next insures a smoother transition from one phase of your life to another. Perform today and plan ahead for the challenges of tomorrow, because in most cases, tomorrow is right around the corner. There are challenges there too. You might think you have the world by the tail you're 15 or 18 or 21 but beyond those days are challenges that can be difficult to imagine. There is college. What career path will you choose? There are jobs, both rewarding and challenging. There are interpersonal relationships that can secure your course or upset it. At times the possibilities can seem endless and daunting.

Take it one step at a time and soon you'll be 30 (Good Lord – 30!) and it doesn't stop there. You'll need to think about buying a house, starting a family, raising kids to be productive adults. You'll take a quick look back and maybe make some changes. You'll start saving for retirement. Yes that day will come after a long progression of events, choices, changes and challenges.

Your approach to your future will depend on your outlook and attitude. Your future will be largely determined by your choices today. Try to do something each day that will impact tomorrow and the next day. Make your life matter.

CHAPTER 6

STOP AND THINK FIRST

Planning for tomorrow and the next day requires thought and a workable plan. The operative word is "workable." Think First. Do Next. Accomplish one thing at a time, then move on to the next task. There will be times when multitasking will be necessary. Sometimes that works. Sometimes, not so much. Like building a house, you lay the foundation first and proceed from there.

Plan, yes, but don't overthink it. Dwelling on a subject can blind a person to the other options available. Fixating on a goal can cloud your judgment and prevent you from entertaining a solution that might work better. Make a mental list of the objective and the available, reasonable options. The operative word here is reasonable. Rushing headlong into a solution that may just get you by, may not be as effective as a little more thought, perhaps from a different perspective that would give you a better, longer lasting, more effective result.

Sometimes it's the difference between a Reaction and a Response. There is a world of difference in both the process and the result. A reaction is sometimes referred to as a knee-jerk, while a response is more often, better thought out. It may take a little longer to appreciate the result but the reward at completion is well worth the effort. Again, there is an operative word. In this case, it's Effort. Most things that bring a good result, require a concerted effort at some, maybe all stages in the process. It's the old adage of earn, then have. Few rewards just fall into our laps without effort, without thought or planning and sometimes even without just a little luck.

CHAPTER 7

PROCRASTINATION

Putting off until tomorrow what you can do today is rarely a good idea because duties and responsibilities tend to accumulate while you wait for circumstances to change. That just means you will have that much more to consider and do the next time or later. More in this case is NOT better. It's just more.

Procrastination can creep into our daily lives, basically unnoticed and certainly unheralded. It can start during childhood. The reasons are usually pretty well hidden. Most of us had jobs to do as kids. Clean your room. Clean the basement. Shovel the driveway. (for kids who grew up in Wisconsin) We'd put it off as long as we could and then dad would come home from work. Your room was a mess. There were your little brother's toys all over the basement and dad couldn't get in the driveway because the snow was still there and was now 15 inches deep. Where were you in this scenario? You were building a snow fort with the neighborhood kids. You had waited too long. You had tempted fate and now you were in trouble. That was your introduction to procrastination, and you had never even heard the word.

Then you got a little older and getting things done in a timely manner took on a new meaning. You had a paper route or a job helping an elderly neighbor and there was money involved. Mowing the neighbor's yard was the ticket to whatever you wanted to do on Saturday because you had a $5.00 bill burning a hole in your pocket, but old habits die hard. You waited and then saw the neighbor kid mowing Mr. Miller's yard. Another lesson was learned.

Soon you were in High School and College. Term papers had deadlines. Part time jobs had time clocks and girls didn't want to wait forever to be asked out on a date. Now you were paying attention to using your time to your advantage. Using your time wisely became a priority. You were learning.

There would still be time when procrastination would creep into your life but you were older and wiser now and the consequences had gotten your attention.

Keep your eye on the ball and watch for opportunities. Balance priorities and have a plan each day. Life will be less complicated that way and you'll enjoy the journey more.

CHAPTER 8

FRIENDSHIPS

It's not a particularly big word but it's among the most important concepts in the English language and in life. A friend is different than an acquaintance but the two are often confused. When my son was 5 or 6 and he forgot or just didn't know another boy's name, he simply said, "come on friend. Let's play." He was too young to differentiate between who was a friend and who was not. Friendship is earned, through time or circumstance, trial or things that you may have in common.

Classmates or teammates can begin as acquaintances and end up as friends. A writer named Brian Chalker put it best. "Friends are for a Reason, a Season or a Lifetime." They are often experienced separately but sometimes experienced simultaneously or in quick succession. I worked with my friend Jim in a maximum-security prison for 14 years. We faced quiet, sometimes routine days, long, dark nights, aggravated assaults and stabbings and two full scale prison riots. Jim started in Custody, as a correction officer and retired as a deputy warden. I started in Treatment as a nurse and then as a psychiatric social worker. I've seen both the look of fear and the look of confidence on his face and he has seen both on mine. Away from the job, we've shared weddings and funerals of family members and friends, fishing, cutting firewood and watching the steam rise from our coffee cups early in the morning. We are still friends, now 40 years later and I could call Jim tomorrow at 2 AM and he wouldn't say "what's wrong?" he'd say, "I'll be right there" and I'd do the same for him. The friendship was all three, a reason, a season and I guess we could say for a lifetime. It doesn't get much better than that.

My locker partner in high school and I began as acquaintances and ended up as friends. Like many friendships, it evolved through school, military service, careers in law enforcement and well into retirement. Now, we still talk on the phone, exchange e-mails and get together with our wives once or twice a year, now that we live on opposite ends of the country. For most of the last 60 years, Tim and I have been friends. I'd do most anything for him and the feeling is mutual. The value placed on earned friendship is different or next to impossible to quantify. Sometimes it just IS and we are grateful for that.

You'll often hear the term "Best Friend," but don't be fooled by the magnitude or longevity of the term. In many cases a best friend is a fleeting experience. Your best friend in the neighborhood you grew up in may not be your best friend in school. When you get to high school the field of possibilities is wide open and the friends of your childhood may fade into the past. Don't feel bad and don't try to cling unrealistically to Bobby from Hargrove St. or Ted from 7th grade. Each of those relationships is valuable at the time of experience but very little in life is permanent, especially when people, experience and geography are concerned. It takes work to maintain a friendship in any time frame and sometimes factors beyond your control, or with human nature, prevent the friendship from growing beyond its time and distance limitations.

There are friends in need, friends indeed and friends of circumstance. Each has its individual value and dynamic. Be careful and pay attention to the nuances that are indicators of which kind of friendship you are experiencing. I've heard from a couple of my friends, who have weathered the changes with me for 5 or 6 decades, that "Old friends are the best friends." I hope you are lucky enough to experience that phenomenon in person. You will understand then, what this all means.

Then there's the time and circumstance when boy / girl relationships come into play. This as they say, is a whole new ball game. There will be friends, just friends, good friends, boy / girlfriends, school friends and co-workers that you don't see anywhere else, lab partners – not friends, locker partners, teammates, older friends, younger friends, and of course, best friends and your BFF (Best Friend Forever). Bear in mind that "forever" is a negotiable term. There are degrees of friendship, friendships that vary, determined by who else might be in the room or within ear shot. The variety and degree in complexity of your friendships will vary with the passage of time, proximity and circumstance. You can also have more than one "best friend" at a time, subject to the same variations.

Proximity and caliber of friendships are worth mentioning in relation to the phrase "keep your friends close and your enemies closer." Sometimes you'll have to disguise your true feelings toward someone in order to protect a confidence or ideal until a situation passes or is resolved. As the saying goes, "it's complicated." Sometimes it's important to step back and view a friendship through more objective eyes, and sometimes you must proceed with caution, in order to protect someone who might get caught in the middle of a fight or misunderstanding, not of their making.

The older you get, the more important friends and friendships can become. Something as simple as having someone to share breakfast with or a cup of coffee on the workbench or a story or an experience can make the day of an older person or a person experiencing trauma or loss. It can make the difference between a mediocre day, a bad day, or a good day.

The intensity can change when your friend who is a boy or girl becomes a boyfriend or girlfriend. The dynamic can change either abruptly or over time and there is seldom a way to predict progress or pace. That, however, is a conversation for another time and place. Once again, when it comes to friends and friendships, be kind, patient and understanding. It will pay big dividends as time passes and experiences lead you through the forest of friendships.

CHAPTER 9

THE ONLY CONSTANT IS CHANGE

Yes, change, in all its forms and instances is inevitable. There are changes that you will experience that will affect you only slightly and changes that will rock your world and alter the way you look at the people and events around you.

When you were very young, you weren't aware of that which was changing around you. Your powers of perception and memory were not yet fully developed. You were at the mercy of circumstance and the adults who were guiding the events that impacted your young life on a daily basis. They guarded you, fed you and clothed you and saw to it that your needs were met. It's what your parents and those entrusted with your care did while you developed.

At the same time, society was changing, sometimes for the better, sometimes not. The things that were taught in school went far beyond reading, writing and math. Society imposed a new normal, new education, new ways of raising and disciplining children. Spanking or any other kind of physical discipline became socially unacceptable. In the 1940's, 50's, 60's and into the 70's, spanking was considered "corrective." Today it's considered abuse or assault. In 25 or 30 years, we'll see how that worked out. Without some sort of discipline, there may well be no consequences for inappropriate or hurtful behavior.

Children of today (the early 2020's) tend to feel more "entitled" to everything the world has to offer. That in itself is a significant change. The concept of discipline and control has changed significantly, hopefully for the betterment of society...but historically, societies that evolved into permissive excess, like the Roman Empire, soon or later evolve into chaos and ultimately fail, taken over by a more disciplined, more rigid society with more rigid rules and greater consequences for those who refuse to "comply" with the new order of things. The jury is still out for the American society here in the United States. A good example of this decline into chaos would be the riots of the summer of 2020 where billions of dollars of property were damaged or destroyed, scores of police were injured or killed and nobody faced any consequences for the actions of the rioters. Still today, at the end of 2022, gangs of youth are breaking into luxury goods stores, smashing display cases and stealing high dollar merchandise without consequence. California has enacted a policy that states that if you steal under $900.00 in value, you will not be prosecuted or even arrested. Some large cities have enacted "no cash bail" policies which allow you to commit a crime in the evening and you are released back into society by the next day with no visible consequences. There are today, thousands of illegal immigrants crossing our southern border each day from more than 50 countries all over the world. Our government appears to be powerless by circumstance or by design, allowing illegal drugs and people to enter our country. They are provided with cell phones, lodging, medical care and education with no tangible investment on their part. The illegal drugs are killing upwards of 300 US citizens per day and our government stands silent in the face of the assault. This is the chaos that could precede the collapse of our society. Watch it as it develops and see if anyone steps in to change the course of history. The show will be worth the price of admission.

Let's take a step back here. As you grow into your elementary school years, you play a more active role. You start making decisions within the events that occur around you. You can decide to walk or to run, to concentrate on your homework or your cell phone, the television, your I-pad, or social media. Decisions are still relatively simple, but you have a degree of influence. It develops as you grow up. You are becoming an agent of change. The choices of some, have been discussed in previous pages. What will your choices be?

Your decisions now carry more weight and the changes that went along with those decisions were often accompanied by an altered circumstance or the decisions and or actions of others. You met the "others" in the previous paragraphs. Your family might move to another town as their lives and jobs change and you change schools, change friends, teachers, neighborhoods, part time jobs and activities.

You are still vulnerable to the changes made by others but within that set of circumstances, you change as well. Your thoughts mature and you began to make independent choices based on a young maturing mind. You start to choose activities, interests and friends, some of or all of which are changes based on changing circumstances.

The older you get, the more control you have over your choices and the impact of the changes have on your day-to-day life. You'll hear the phrases like "go with the flow" or "don't buck the system." You'll be able to decide whether you are a leader or a follower and how much you want to be an agent of change in your own life or in the lives of others. You'll learn that developmental change can be a good thing and you can take advantage of opportunities to make progress. Or you can dig your heels in and resist the inevitable changes that are taking place. It will now largely be your choice.

A good example of inevitable change is the change in activity and interests among the nation's youth. I'll take you on a short trip in the "way back machine" to demonstrate the magnitude of the change.

When I grew up on Hargrove Street in the 1950s and 1960s, there were probably 20 some kids living in the 25 or 30 houses, all built shortly after World War II. Someone asked me, not long ago, "what was important to you when you were 10? My response was simple. Was the ice on the lake thick enough to skate on? Was it too windy to go fishing and were there enough kids to play baseball? It all sounds pretty simplistic today and none of those 3 are probably important to the 10-year-olds of today. Today you don't see kids in the summertime.

They stay indoors on their laptops, I-phones, social media outlets like Twitter and Facebook and an incredible array of electronic options. The baseball diamonds that we created on vacant lots have disappeared. Kids don't skate on the lake or fish at the mouth of the creek or ride their bikes around the lake, a distance of about 10 miles. The gaggle of kids at the school bus stop is replaced by a line of cars, waiting to discharge their passengers or pick them up after school. God forbid that anybody would walk to school or ride their bike. It just wouldn't be cool, and they might be teased or thought less of by their classmates.

If you lived less than 2 miles from school, you walked or rode your bike unless it was raining. Bus stops were safer, and parents worried less. The term "helicopter parent" hadn't been invented yet. It was a safer time, to be sure. Compare that to the children and their habits today. The changes are inevitable, and the children of tomorrow will look back (or maybe not) and notice their own evolution. I hope they're willing and able to see the change and adjust accordingly.

Sometimes change requires risk. The simple act of trying something that you've never done before involves risk. You muster the knowledge and skill that you've acquired along the way so far and you try something new, like water skiing or rock climbing. There will be times when the change you make will work against you. Again, a change requires that you adapt to that which is new. When this happens, stop and think. Explore your options. You may have several or you may have only one that will work to your advantage. Don't be afraid to change. It may be in your best interest. Try to avoid obsessing on a bad situation. Use the experience, even the negative experience, to learn the art of positive change.

As you plunge into and through puberty, your choices and changes will become more complex and will carry consequences not noticed when you were in the single digits. Life is becoming more complicated, faster and requiring greater attention to detail.

Then you'll discover girls (or boys) and life will never be the same. Relationships require attention, patience, and the ability to appreciate the thoughts and feelings of others. Dating adds a new dimension to an already complicated existence as a teenager. Hormones and emotions can run wild and can be more confusing. There is an adage that goes like this: "Intellect over Emotion." It requires a conscious decision to think with your brain, not with your heart. The two can work well together but with all the other changes that are taking place at the same time, you will have to think first, feel second and act, third.

Change is a never-ending process. It will be a constant companion throughout your life. You'll decide whether to go to college, what college? Trade school? The Military or employment? What apartment? How will you save money (or will you save money?) Will you ask her to go steady or to marry you? Will you smoke or not? Will you use drugs? Will you take the job that pays the most (right now) or the job that has a better future? Will you buy a house or rent or move to another town where the opportunities are greater? Will you save for your retirement from the beginning of your work life, or will you wait (because I need ALL my money NOW!) Your decisions are important. Treat them as such.

As you can see, changes will accompany you through your entire life and decisions will grow in importance as the years pass. ....
BUT!............ There are some things that will seemingly and hopefully, NEVER CHANGE. It's Christmas time and in October we start hearing Christmas music in the stores. It seems to creep in a week earlier every

couple of years and that leads us to the NEVER part of this narrative. Some of the songs and their singers have weathered the pressures and politics of time.

Some of those singers you've probably never heard of, like Gene Autry singing Rudolph the Red Nosed Reindeer or Andy Williams singing Oh Holy Night or Bing Crosby singing White Christmas or Burl Ives singing It's a Holly Jolly Christmas. All those singers are dead but some of those recordings have been played since the 1940's. If the Woke / Cancel Culture has its way, they will all be canceled in deference to the politically vocal minority that wants to change the name of Christmas to "Winter Holiday" and change it to a strictly secular event. (Please, don't let them do it.) With any luck, the cancel culture mob will all see the error of their ways or be eaten by fire ants and field mice. You will probably witness their awful behavior. Be strong and resist. All change is not good, but change is inevitable.

CHAPTER 10

OPEN DISCUSSION VS. ARGUMENT

Communication takes many forms. There's being told what to do by a parent, a teacher or a supervisor. There are questions and answers to clarify that type of exchange. There are cries for help, expressions of anger or grief or joy. They are all normal parts of communication in our lives. When an issue arises that needs clarification or that you disagree with, you have options. You can choose to talk about it, exchanging ideas, with both or all concerned approaching the issue with open minds, discussing the pros and cons until you agree on an approach that guarantees an acceptable result...OR...you can dig your heels in, unwilling to see it from another perspective and close your mind to the possibility of compromising or changing your mind. The discussion becomes an argument in which nobody is flexible or willing to "listen" to the other point of view. Voices rise in pitch and volume and active listening stops. Progress and possible resolution are no longer on the table. Friendships can be altered or lost, and the issue is left unchanged, causing frustration and division between those involved. Small issues can become major problems that can last for weeks, months or even years.

Active listening is the key to success in resolving a heated issue. Labor-Management conferences, political debates and developing contentious interaction can all be handled successfully if all parties listen to each other. Yes, the operative term is "Listen."

CHAPTER 11

TAKING CARE OF YOURSELF
WANT VS. NEED / EARN / HAVE

Taking care of yourself can go in one of two directions. You must ask yourself if your decision is made from selfishness or survival or somewhere in between. Decisions involve insight into both the situation before you and the long-range result of your behavior choices.

You're in a convenience store with a schoolmate. You see him pocket two candy bars, one for himself and maybe one for you, because he wasn't a chicken, afraid to get caught and you were. Here's where your youthful survival instinct comes into play. Do you walk away, leaving your buddy with the goods, or do you watch him as he exits the store under the watchful eye of the camera in the corner, and share the take.

It boils down to a couple things. Is the risk worth the reward OR potential consequences and does the want override the need? Scenarios similar to this will crop up in different contexts throughout your life. The risk / reward, want / need are repetitive occurrences. Do you look at the test paper of the person next to you when the teacher isn't looking? Do you plagiarize a report or do you do your own research and writing? Do you get in a car with your buddies, knowing that there will be beer, booze or drugs in the car? Do you "use" or not? Do you lie when you get in a jam, knowing that someone else will be blamed for your actions? Will you get caught? Can your reputation or that of someone else be damaged? Let's go back to "will you get caught"? It might be among the first considerations. Maybe not.

The county jails and state prisons are full of inmates who thought, "I'll never get caught because I'm smarter than they are." We're back to Risk / Reward. Is the risk worth the potential consequences? The risk goes up as the choices made poorly grow from candy bars to toys and tools to drugs and police cars. Sooner or later, you'll pay a price for your poor decisions.

You will be put in a position to be your own best friend or your own worst enemy. Opting out of a potentially dangerous situation can pay dividends both in the moment and in the future. Future employers will do a background investigation before they hire you. The blemish of a police record or something you put on Facebook or Twitter can cast a long shadow and can prevent you from getting a career producing job. For 10 years, 20 years or more, it can follow you, now in the age of computers and Artificial Intelligence. Some records are forever, so exercising responsibility for yourself is a good exercise in judgment.

It boils down to personal values, the standards by which you were raised and the standards you choose to live by. Ask yourself, "what is my reputation and time worth when I'm facing consequences. Are you thinking in the present, chasing instant gratification, or the future.... or neither? I asked one of my patients, age 22, in my office in the prison hospital, how much time he was doing for selling cocaine on the streets of Hartford, Connecticut. His reply was, "I'm just doing a quick nickel." That's 5 years by the calendar. It caught me just a little off guard because the value he put on his time was no greater than the bicycle he stole when he was 10. He was a busy corner drug dealer and years later, when I asked him what he wanted to do when he got out of prison, he said without hesitation, "I'm going to take my corner back." He knew that another drug dealer had filled his position on the corner when he went to prison, but that didn't appear to faze him in the least. He hadn't measured the risk or the consequences. He knew he wasn't going to get caught......But he did......again.

He had lost sight of his own value and values and had forgotten his standards, if he in fact had ever had any. His poor decisions were based on want instead of need. Consequences were never considered and a new somebody else is selling drugs on his corner today. It is no longer HIS corner.

There is a kinder, less selfish, more productive way to take care of yourself. It involves rewarding yourself for hard work, for accomplishing your goals and for a job well done. In some circles it's called R & R (Rest and Relaxation). It's a necessary element in maintaining "balance" physically, practically and emotionally. The alternative is exhaustion in one or all these areas. It's healthy to rest, to reward yourself and recuperate. Movies, sports, exercise, time spent with friends, laughter and the occasional afternoon nap can work wonders in rekindling your energy for the tasks and activities ahead. Time with friends, time to quietly reflect while alone (or time contemplating your navel) are all important. Family support, fishing with your dad or puttering with your grandfather or helping a younger brother with a project, all can make a difference in your ability and willingness to take on the next challenge. Taking care of yourself and recharging your batteries isn't selfish. It's survival and plays a vital role in your day-to-day life.

CHAPTER 12

YOU DON'T ALWAYS HAVE TO BE RIGHT
YOU DON'T HAVE TO BE PERFECT

Using your best judgement doesn't guarantee that you'll be right all the time. We learn as we go and sometimes, we learn the hard way. Nobody knows it all. Remember that. It's important. There are gaps in everyone's learning history, depending on your interests, education, opportunities, your personality and a host of other factors. Our credibility is not based on being right. It's based on your honest effort to use facts to back up your statements, but circumstances change, and your statements may require a change based on newly acquired information.

If we were all perfect, there would be no merit to trying harder. It would all be for show and after a time, your friends and acquaintances, peers and co-workers could begin to think they don't have anything to offer to the relationship and would begin to feel alienated or even bored. Perfection may be important in a recital or the climax of great effort or in surgery, but perpetual perfection in everyday life can set you apart in a negative way. Attempts to appear perfect can be alienating, not uniting. Perfection may be well represented by the perfect touchdown pass or a perfect dive from the 3-meter board, but many of those are singular and fleeting victories. An activity or sport performed as a team may well include efforts that don't individually display perfection but may well contribute to the ultimate success of the team. There are times when victory shared by many outshines the perfect performance of one individual.

CHAPTER 13

IT'S A SMALL, SMALL WORLD......REALLY

And it's more than a Disney exhibit theme song. As time passes and technology improves, the world gets smaller every day. Life is a learning journey and along your journey you will meet, study with, play with and work with many kinds of people. Some you will like. Some you will appreciate or admire and some you will barely be able to tolerate. It's the last category that will require the most attention because when you least expect it, you may well see those people again in the years ahead.

The co-worker or supervisor you cross or lie to or tangle with when you are a new employee may be your boss again, down the road. The police lieutenant you reported for handling an arrest over aggressively, may one day be the shift commander or your police chief in the years to come. The girl or boy you lied to or lied about in high school may become the director of human resources in a company you would like to work for. The list goes on and on. Companies can be international and reputations matter. Yours is worth protecting. It will become more so, as time passes, and you become more well known within your career field. When you get promoted and you meet the same person that you crossed swords with, in years past and he or she now runs the company, you want that first-handshake in many years to be welcoming. It will all be up to you, today. Don't miss the opportunity to leave a positive impression, even if you are leaving one position for another, in another company. Some burned bridges cannot be repaired. Don't lose sight of that fact.

CHAPTER 14

THE LONG DOLLAR

I received two very important pieces of advice when I was in my early teens. In and around other words of wisdom, my dad told me to keep my eye on what he called "The Long Dollar." To him it was important to teach his children the value of honest work and saving money for the days ahead. For him, payday wasn't necessarily the best day to let that check burn a hole in his pocket. His advice was to put ¼ of your pay in a savings account and if you were working (even a part time, after school job), give your mom $10.00 a week for cooking and cleaning and washing your clothes. He acknowledged that it might seem like a lot of money to put in two places when I was only making 60 cents /hour as a 13-year-old janitor at our church school after school, but he promised me it would instill financial discipline in me that would pay dividends in the years ahead. I couldn't see it then, but looking back, he was right. All I wanted to do was to be able to buy my own shoes, so I didn't have to wear brown Boy Scout shoes anymore. There wasn't a lot of money in our house in the 1960's with 7 kids in the house. I had to learn to save whatever was left of my meager paycheck until I could afford those shoes. I saved and learned the value of "earned money." It was my first lesson in earn / have.

I also learned to separate Want from Need. It wasn't always an easy lesson. I quickly learned that there were a lot of things that I wanted and not nearly as many things that I needed. My brother John was much better at saving than I was. He probably still is. Separating want from need was a valuable lesson that I've worked on often in the years since. I think it's an acquired skill for some of us. Some skills come naturally, and some take more practice.

The second life lesson was taught by my grandfather. When I was 16, he asked me where I saw myself in five years. Grandpa Duckert was a wise and thoughtful, quiet man and his question surprised me. He I was a sophomore in high school without a firm grasp on my future. The options were both open and endless, so I admitted that I didn't know. He said two things. He said, "Go to college and when you choose an occupation work for the government, either county, state or federal, because they will be the only jobs that will have genuine pension plans when you get ready to retire. Once again, the long dollar was in play. Now, 60 years after that advice was given, I've lived to be grateful for it. I've learned to save part of each paycheck for when I would need funds most and I retired from the State of Connecticut, Dept. of Corrections after nearly 25 years of service and earned that coveted pension.

In retrospect, Grandpa Duckert was right. Most pension plans have been discontinued due to company or corporate budget constraints and have been converted to something that resembles a 401 K plan or some other plan that is vulnerable to economic swings. Thanks Dad and Thanks Grandpa Duckert. This goes back to an earlier chapter, "Listen To The Old Men."

CHAPTER 15

FREEDOM ISN'T FREE.

Listening to the wisdom of older men and women pays dividends in other ways, separate from financial considerations. I had to learn that as I grew up. Your world will open with many options, opportunities, obligations and responsibilities that only increase as you age. From responsibility for yourself, to that of your family, your job, your community and your country, your circle of activity and influence grows.

One of those options is military service. As times change, attitudes change toward the military. Fewer young people feel any sense of obligation to serve in any of the armed forces. In some families, it is looked on as a tradition, in some as an obligation and others still, it is looked on as an inconvenience. One way to look at it goes like this. You can't graduate without studying. You can't buy a car without paying for it. You can't earn interest without saving or investing. You can't get something for nothing without having it given to you or stealing it. You can't legitimately enjoy freedom without playing a role in the maintenance of it. Freedom Isn't Free.

The bottom line is simple. We are a country that requires its citizens to invest in its success to sustain that which we have. That concept is exclusive of the portion of the population that chooses to live off the government dole and live off the efforts and investments of others.

Many of us have grandfathers who served in World War I, fathers who served in World War II, or the Korean War. We have brothers, sons and friends who served in Viet Nam, Iraq and Afghanistan. There never seems to be a shortage of world conflicts to occupy our youth to protect the concept of peace on our shores.

My family is littered with military veterans from Grandpa Duckert to my dad, to four of my brothers, my son and me. It was both an obligation, an opportunity and a privilege to know that we took part in the greatest adventure and the greatest opportunity to contribute to the stability and success of our country. None of us would trade the experience for anything. It was an opportunity to be a part of something much bigger than us. There is no greater obligation or experience to look back on and say, "Wow! I was part of that effort." Every time you see the American flag raised or hear or sing the National Anthe or Pledge of Allegiance, you'll get a lump in your throat or a tear in your eye, remembering the people you served with and people who served before you. There is no feeling that can be compared and no feeling that you can share with another human being, that means more.

Military service isn't glamorous or glorious. It can be hard work, sometimes dangerous and sometimes it will seem like a long haul but investing in the safety of your country and your relatives and friends and even perfect strangers carries with it a sense of pride that you won't find anywhere else.

Make a difference.

CHAPTER 16

LEARN TO WALK, THEN TO RUN

Most people were not born with infinite knowledge or patience. We usually learn as we go. As teenagers, you may go through a period where you think that your parents and anyone over the age of 20 are out of touch and stupid. Worry not. The older you get, the more you will rethink that mindset and when you're in your twenties, you'll wonder how your dad got so smart, suddenly. As your ambitions and goals become more career oriented, you'll start to experiment with different approaches to problems. Don't be afraid to try small steps first. The giant leaps will come on their own. It's much like a NASCAR race. They start by "qualifying" to see in what order the drivers will start the race. Each position is earned. As the laps tick off, they adjust their race cars to run faster and better in the hope that they will be in front when the checkered flag flies. They get to know the track and their competition better as they go. Your journey through life may well see that pattern appear again and again.

Almost all of life's endeavors are learned in stages. Pee Wee Football, Little League Baseball, Junior Varsity first then Varsity. As you pass through the stages, you perfect the techniques necessary to be successful. There are musical prodigies who somehow can play the violin or the piano at age 4 or 5, but that is not the norm. We learn mostly by experience. The more we practice, the better we can become. Like most things in life, it's a process. Don't be afraid of it or bored by it. Embrace it.

CHAPTER 17

EVERYBODY MAKES MISTAKES

...Except those who don't try. They live in a hollow paradise, wondering why others progress, and they seem to be stuck in place and or time. The old saying is "To err is human." Each of us is different, different in many ways, and it's supposed to be that way. Some people are good at detail. Their calculations always seem to be spot on. The kid sitting next to that person makes mistakes in calculation and comes up with the wrong answer and a red check mark. How you address the mistake is what matters.

There are errors in judgement when you think a person is one way and you are rudely awakened to find out they are totally different. We make mistakes of choice when it comes to behavior. Should we experiment with pot or with hash or meth or heroine? In retrospect, when you're sitting in the back of a police cruiser, you think, "Ya! That was a mistake." Mistakes come in all sizes, large and small. The consequences that can follow can be of the same magnitude, both large and small, long term or of short duration.

One of the biggest mistakes is fooling yourself, thinking, it doesn't really matter, or I won't get caught. In real life, it DOES really matter and only a fool goes through life thinking he won't get caught.

Mistakes are made in relationships as well. We'll think someone is our girlfriend or boyfriend, only to see them hand-in-hand with someone else. Confronting them in public might be a mistake. Letting it simmer while you become more upset may only make matters worse. Sometimes there is no solution other than time and distance to realign your perspective.

We might think that someone understands the issue, but we haven't identified or explained the issue leaving the other person in the dark with insufficient information. Hence, misunderstandings can boil over into angry confrontations and everybody gets hurt in the process.

After you've become aware of your mistakes, you have some options. You can ignore what is sometimes known as the elephant in the room. That usually makes the matter worse and the resolution farther away. You can lie about it and refuse to admit that you made the mistake. Soon enough, you will discover the folly of that tactic, when the end result comes crashing down on you from a source that you didn't expect. The best way to handle it is to admit to it. Don't be afraid to say, "I screwed up. How can I help fix it"? That opens a new and much more productive dialogue and the chances of resolving the problem become exponentially better. If you get stuck, trying to resolve a mistake, find somebody to talk to about it. A fresh, perhaps more objective perspective may be the answer because when we make a mistake, we sometimes panic and that immobilizes our thought process to a greater or lesser degree. Keep in mind that nearly all mistakes are recoverable. Don't be afraid to make the effort.

CHAPTER 18

BUMPS IN THE ROAD

Yes, there will be bumps along the road, whether you are rich or poor, socially in tune or awkward around others. When you don't make the football team or are second string in baseball, you will feel the bumps. They are a part of real life. When you can't get the course you want in school or when you realize that your boyfriend / girlfriend isn't that into you or when your job application sits in somebody's in-box for a month, because it just doesn't "pop", or you get laid off from a job that you really like, due to budget constraints, you have choices on how to handle the disappointment. You come to grips with the theory that loss and frustration and even failure are facts of life. It unfortunately does not stop in high school and college.

When you face professional or heavily credentialed paraprofessional competition, you realize quickly that you may well be a small fish in a big pond. Most career pathways don't care that you were the fullback on your high school football team or the head cheerleader who dated the jock or the rich guy who always seemed to have money and a car. Human Resource Managers want to know what your grades were like, what kind of extracurricular activities you were involved in and what you have accomplished between then and now. What were you like at your last job? What kind of employee were you?

Then, after 5 or 6 years of feeling pretty comfortable in your mid-level position, there is a major reduction in staff, and you are getting "bumped" by somebody who knows nothing about your job but has more seniority in the company. It's a gut-punch and can either send you into a tailspin or propel you into exploring another option.

It's always good to have a plan "B", no matter what your position or job is. It's career survival and, yes, this could happen to you. That's the reason that many of our military personnel have both a Primary Military Occupational Specialty (MOS) and a Secondary MOS, often not necessarily in the same career field. The equivalent is a college major and a minor course of study. It pays to have more than one area of interest or pursuit to make the bumps in the road a little less problematic.

It can be difficult to navigate the quagmire of personality and administrative politics, and you'll find that it can plague you for years until the person who causes the dissension either leaves under his own power or is asked to vacate his position. You're going to work with (or against) people you don't like and people who don't like or respect you. Take heart in that you are probably not the first victim of his or her disdain. I'd love for it to be different, but it's not.

I like it when those in upper management, who pull the occupational strings, say emphatically that this is a "character building experience." Just in case there was one smidgen of truth in that statement, don't believe a word of it. Although on rare occasions it works to your ultimate advantage, the basic premise is pure garbage. You're still "fired, laid off or otherwise no longer needed." Learn to roll with the punches, always have a plan "B" and be ready for the bumps in the road.

CHAPTER 19

DON'T GROW UP TOO FAST

Enjoy being a kid. Embrace each new experience as it comes. You'll only be a teenager once and there are many things to learn along the way. Each lesson helps prepare you for the challenges ahead. Don't spend a lot of time wishing you were 18 or wishing you could go back to being 14, before you had to shoulder the responsibilities of an adult. Life is a learning journey where you build your fund of knowledge as you go.

Along the road, be mindful of the small things, things that many of your peers will fail to notice. Sometimes it's the small and seemingly insignificant things that make the difference between success and failure.

Accomplish "Something" every day, for yourself and for someone else. By the time you sit down for breakfast you have had an opportunity already. Make your bed. It's your first accomplishment and a good way to begin your conquest of the day. It's also good to look at a nicely made bed when you're ready to end your day, knowing that you started your day with an accomplishment (and your mom didn't have to do it for you.)

Each day is full of opportunities to accomplish things in a big way or small way. They all matter to someone. Often your efforts will go unnoticed. That's reality. Get used to it, but small gestures done for others can make the day for an elderly person or a person with fewer resources. The recipient of your kindness may not know who helped them or why, but you'll know that you made a difference, and that feeling is hard to beat.

CHAPTER 20

THAT WHICH WAS LEFT UNSAID

In real estate the saying is Location-Location-Location, when they describe what is most important in their business. It's probably a true statement. In human interaction, it can safely be said that the 3 most important things are Communication-Communication-Communication. The world of human interaction at all ages revolves around that interpersonal exchange of information. There are many ways to communicate, each with its own set of advantages and disadvantages. Timing, content, context and inflection are each important. The ability to convey a message effectively is an important skill to acquire sooner than later. What is said is sometimes compromised by How it is said and there are times that you will have to read between the lines and listen to that which is NOT SAID.

Over time, you'll hear the phrase "The Elephant in the Room." The elephant is that subject that needs to be addressed but you are either reluctant or afraid to talk about it. It's probably more common between couples who are in long term relationships or between parents and children of divorce, or in small groups that may not share the same goals. The elephant can make or break a relationship or allow it to die a natural death.

Talking about the elephant can clear the air, allowing all those concerned to resolve their doubts and clear the air or walk away, knowing that they've done all they can do. If you know that you can't change the status quo, it is sometimes wise to leave well enough alone but, in most cases, resolution of an issue or problem leaves all concerned in a better place and more trusting in the relationship.

There are letters, notes, books and texts, phone calls, telegrams and love notes. There are loud voices, soft voices and lyrics to songs that "speak to you" in one way or another. Each has a time and a place in which it is most effectively used to communicate.

You might be tempted to use a corner of truth to shed light on a message that may well be far from the whole truth. You may be tempted to cloud an exchange with fluff or a smoke screen to cover up the real story or the real meaning. It's called verbal sleight of hand and is designed to deceive the other person or group of people. Politicians use it all the time. In recent speech to a group of abortion rights activists in Georgia, Vice President Harris made a profound point to the eager crowd that "our constitution guarantees us Liberty and the Pursuit of Happiness." She left out the word Life because she was speaking to a group that supports abortion. That was an example of verbal sleight of hand. It's one of the reasons that when a person is sworn in as a witness in a court trial, they respond to "Do you swear to speak the truth, the WHOLE TRUTH and nothing but the truth. The little corner of truth simply won't do in a court of law. Using this tactic will ultimately catch up with you and will damage your credibility. When caught in this kind of deception, people no longer trust you and when trust is lost, the relationship is irreparably damaged. It doesn't mean that you should bore a person with meaningless details, but sharing important, meaningful information on a regular basis allows people to trust that you are a credible person and are engaged in the relationship.

The same rule applies to limiting that which you tell your significant other. Whether the relationship is between boyfriend-girlfriend, friend to friend or husband and wife, willing openness ensures the absence of misunderstanding and supports a trusting relationship. It also ensures the negative response to the ill fated "Oh, By The Way" when he or she has to divulge a long held secret that could alter the strength of a relationship. This is particularly important when dealing with the elephant in the room.

There will be times when you want to "say something" and you just don't know how it will be received or it's a feeling that you want to share but don't know how to say it. In a case like this, make the effort if that which would be left unsaid, would help a situation or clarify a feeling toward another person.

Sometimes, telling someone, be it a parent or a child, a partner or a friend, how much they mean to you, could make their day or reinforce the way they feel about you. Leaving it unsaid could lead to misunderstanding or feeling unfulfilled. That could be perceived as apathy and lead to the premature or unnecessary dissolution of a relationship. The bottom line is, if you think it might help or if the feeling is so strong that it hurts, take the risk and say it, gently, and sincerely but firmly where necessary.

CHAPTER 21

LIFE IS NOT FAIR

To expect life to be fair (on its own merits) is living in a fool's paradise or being hopelessly naïve. When in grade school and you are blamed for something that you were not a part of, you cry "That's Not Fair." You are absolutely correct. It isn't hair but it IS the reality in which we live. When you get blamed for something your brother did and he won't own up to it, it isn't fair, either. You feel wronged, but you know that there's precious little you can do about it. You can choose to hold a grudge, or you can be alert to it happening again or you can move on, a little wiser for the experience. When your best friend has a new best friend, you think to yourself, "That's Not Fair! I didn't do anything." Maybe that's the problem. Maybe you could have been a better friend or maybe it was a natural turn of events. Your friend may have moved on for any number of reasons, best known to him or herself. Again, it may feel like it's not fair, but life isn't always fair.

In personal interaction on any or many levels, things change. People change. Circumstances change. Geography and attitudes change and often it feels like it isn't fair to be the recipient of the result of that change. It *isn't Fair* but it is what it is. It's reality.

The older you get, the more observant you become about the reality of fairness or lack thereof. You will face consequences for your behavior, or your poor choices and you may well feel that you were punished unfairly. In some cases, you may be absolutely right but in other cases you will have gotten away with something that negatively impacted someone else. You'll go "Whew!" and the other person will say, "That's not fair!"

You might be in competition with another person for a job or a promotion. There might be several of you vying for the same position and someone with what you think are fewer qualifications gets the job. Inside, you are screaming "That's not fair!" It is, however, the reality with which we must live and work. There could be many reasons, both personal and professional, that led to another person getting the job.

Things may run smoothly for long periods of time and then, suddenly, you get slapped down by fate or circumstance over which you are not in control. As an adult, young or old, you may watch political opponents spar for the same office. One or both may use verbal sleight of hand or out-and-out misrepresentation of the truth to gain an unfair advantage over the other. You'll look at it from the cheap seats and say to yourself, "That's not fair," and once again, you'll be right.

Fairness is largely our responsibility in what may appear to be the narrow view of our own lives. We are responsible to treat others fairly, controlling that which we can control. There will be times when that will feel like a very narrow field of view, but without the effort on our part to control the fairness that we initiate, we lose the ability to be fair to others. In that regard, everybody loses and "That's Not Fair."

CHAPTER 22

SAY WHAT YOU MEAN AND MEAN WHAT YOU SAY

Best To Start With The Truth

To understand this, listen to a politician who is trying to address a questionable policy that he wants passed or a news broadcast with a biased agenda. It is sometimes called "verbal sleight of hand" or selective editing in some circles. The goal is to convince the majority of those listening that what you're trying to sell is a great idea and the whole truth when it is only going to be of benefit to a small or select group or turn the viewer in a particular direction.

When we were kids, we might have called them little white lies. A magician would call it sleight of hand, but as we grew up, their content and intent may well have become more important or consequential to a recipient or an unintended (or intended) victim.

Verbal sleight of hand can be broad based and far reaching. In the summer of 2022, rising inflation was on the minds of many Americans. It was at 9.1%, which compared to previous months, was high. In September it dropped to 8.5% from the August high…but the factors that had produced the 9.1% had changed. Food and fuel, the two expendables that drive most of our economy, had been dropped from the factors that contributed to the overall inflation rate and the statement was made that the inflation rate for September, was "ZERO." That was verbal sleight of hand. What would have been more accurate would be to have said that the inflation rate had dropped by .6%. Zero would be cause for great celebration! Declining by .6% would have been cautiously labeled as "a good sign." The latter is true. The Former, not so much.

This wasn't his first foray into the world of verbal deception. He was getting a reputation for not saying what he meant and not meaning what he said.

They were once called "Little White Lies" as if they weren't important enough to worry about, but if you can get away with the little white lie, your confidence in your own ability to deceive others grows and you become a teller of tall tales. Then, finally, when the stakes are higher and the deception greater, someone will catch you in the lie and your reputation will be damaged or ruined, costing you the trust of family and friends, co-workers and the public may have had in you. News of a bad reputation travels fast. Teachers, bosses, siblings and friends stop trusting you. It's a hard cycle to break and recovering a damaged reputation can be difficult or impossible. It can take years.

So, tell the truth from the beginning, even if there are consequences that accompany bad choices in behavior. Everybody makes mistakes, (Where have you heard that before), feathers the edges of a statement, minimizes or exaggerates to improve the chances of being believed in a questionable situation. It is sometimes called embellishing. So, start out by saying exactly what you mean and mean exactly what you say. It will save you the problem of explaining your sleight of hand to your listener who has acted on what you have said, thinking that it meant something other than what you meant. Confusion can be explained and understood. Verbal deception on your part carries consequences when you are found out.

CHAPTER 23

PAY ATTENTION!!

The world we live in is an ever changing, ever evolving place. Be aware of what is going on around you, in your own family, in your school, in your town, in your state and in your country. It's important to Pay Attention.

Changes don't always happen in dynamic ways. Some do, like the election of a new president. Some are quieter, with less fanfare, like the laws enacted by congress in an Omnibus Bill that contains "riders" (extra laws that couldn't get passed on their own merit) to a major piece of legislation. Often the bill isn't even fully read by congress until after it is voted on and becomes the law of the land. It will sneak up on the unsuspecting public with an "oh by the way, there's a hidden ½% tax on a gallon of gas to pay for improvements to infrastructure." (roads and bridges). The congressmen who vote on it and even the public are usually not aware that it is even being considered. You'll hear the term FAT when some of the unsuspected spending is talked about, and now it's the law.

In smaller ways, changes creep into our everyday lives with changes in the way a word is used or in a completely new meaning of an old word. The word "gay" used to be only used in the dark shadows or defined by being happy. Today the word is used proudly and loudly by advocates of an alternative form of sexual expression or lifestyle. An old word can go out of usage, replaced by a more progressive form. A word that was frowned upon by our grandparents and parents is more acceptable and normal and is now called the vernacular.

Take notice that all your friends and family may not think alike on any given issue or event. It doesn't make one or the other right or wrong.

Their opinion (and everybody has one) is probably based on their own history and observation.

One may watch the evening news on mainstream media like NBC, CBS or ABC. One may watch the news on CNN or Fox News or another cable channel. Still others get their news from the internet or social media outlets. The thing to be aware of is that each outlet has a target audience, and each has an agenda. Don't be lulled into believing one agenda or opinion. Watch and listen to several. Notice the differences between them, both obvious and hidden. Then make up your own mind. Think, observe, compare and explore. Look beyond the headlines into that which led up to the headline.

Watch, listen and participate. Watch those around you. Watch the ways they move and the expressions on their faces. Listen to what they say and listen carefully for what they are not saying. Don't be afraid to engage in a conversation AFTER you have given it some thought, sometimes quickly and at other times after collecting more information.

There is a lot going on, both on a small scale, close to home and on a much larger scale, globally, that will impact your life now and, in the days ahead. Pay attention to the details. They are important to your thought process and are the building blocks to the decisions you will make in the future.

CHAPTER 24

TRY TO MAKE A DIFFERENCE

Making a difference can take a combination of thought, circumstance and sometimes planning. There are other times when opportunity drops in your lap and a person in need is standing right in front of you without the ability to act on his or her own.

Making a difference is largely a matter of attitude meeting opportunity. It can require you to take care of yourself first, giving you the resources to assist another person, or it can happen without warning, and you need to react quickly or lose the moment.

It makes no difference whether you are twelve and you're teaching your little brother how to ride a bike or when you're 75 and sharing a cup of coffee on Wednesdays with a nearly blind neighbor who is a shut-in. You are making a difference. As a member of a baseball or soccer team, your contribution to the effort makes a difference, either good or bad. The team effort is the focus.

Without each member contributing his or her own talent and skill, the team will not be successful. In the operating room, it takes more than a talented surgeon to make the operation a success. Each member of the operating team makes an individual and ultimately collective difference. The anesthesiologist puts the patient to sleep so the surgeon can perform the operation. The scrub nurse must know which instrument to hand the surgeon next. The circulating nurse must manage sterile supplies and instrument sets handed to the scrub nurse while maintaining sterility and preventing contamination of the operating field. Each member makes a difference in the success or failure of the operation.

The school play or the spring concert couldn't be pulled off without a host of participants making a difference. The director, the hero or heroine, the lighting crew and the stage crew, the set builders and the supporting cast and the musicians all make a difference. In the military, making a difference is both an individual and a collective effort. Without each member performing his or her assigned duties, trucks would not run. Weapons would not be delivered. Medics could not patch up their wounded, the troops would not get paid, and objectives would not be met.

When you are a part of a collective effort or acting alone, the feeling you get when you know that your contribution mattered is difficult to beat. Pride in a job well done or a task performed well can encourage you or someone else to accomplish even more.

CHAPTER 25

WHAT IS MOST IMPORTANT TO YOU TODAY?

What 3 things are most important to you today? The question can be answered at any age and answered well. Not long ago someone asked me what was important to me when I was 10. I lived near a lake in Wisconsin and that had a bearing on my answer at that young age. My 3 things were: Is the ice thick enough to skate on (in winter), is it too windy to go fishing (in summer) and were there enough kids to play baseball? Today, many years later, it sounds a little selfish but, come on, I was 10. Enough said. Today I'd answer differently because with the passing of time and nearly 77 years old, I'd have to give it more thought, because as we age, our priorities change, and different things are important to us. Today it matters more that my family is safe, that I have things to do that matter to someone besides me and that my truck can get me to and from my shop in the state forest.

Each period, whether brief or long term, has its own priorities and much like best friends (in previous chapter) that which is important to us evolves. It's a way to measure personal growth and a way to adjust to the changes in our lives. Being able to adapt to new circumstances helps us measure what is important today.

What are the 3 most important things to you, Today? Give it some thought.

CHAPTER 26

ADMIT IT WHEN YOU ARE WRONG
AND FIX IT IF YOU CAN

Make a note: NOBODY is right all the time. Our human nature sees to that but admitting that we were wrong can be difficult. Ego can get in the way if we think someone may feel differently toward us or think less of us if we're not perfect.

Having the courage of your convictions is important if that position is researched properly and is based on fact. Don't resort to the S.W.A.G. (Scientific Wild Ass Guess). It is usually a source of confusion or doubt when investigated further. When a conversation ensues and you realize that you sounded like a bonehead, let the listener know that you may have spoken too soon and that you'd like to discuss the matter further. A slightly bruised ego is far better than leading someone astray. It hurts less in the long run, and it can be easier to dig yourself out of a shallow hole than one you dug too deep.

There will be times when you will lack the necessary knowledge to clean up your own speculative mess and someone else will have to fix it. Be gracious and acknowledge their assistance if possible. It could pave the way to further conversation and a better understanding.

On the other hand, if you know you are right and your point of information or opinion is challenged, don't be afraid to defend your position, but know that being right is not always the most important thing. Allowing for an alternative point of view, even one that disagrees with yours, may open the door to a learning experience and may salvage the dignity of another person.

What is right for you may be wrong for someone else and vice versa. It may boil down to a different perspective on the same issue, both of which may render a favorable result, just achieved through different means. There will be times when compromise is possible or wise and sometimes letting someone else be right won't hurt you. It's OK to be neutral in this case. If it can be fixed by a quick correction or even an apology, fix it and move on.

CHAPTER 27

DON'T BE AFRAID TO SAY, I DON'T KNOW

When I passed the state board to get my first nursing license, a wise older nurse (My Mother) gave me some sage advice. She said, "It is far more important to know what you Don't Know than what you do know." It took me a minute to think about that, but as the years passed and I got to work in many different areas of nursing, I realized that there was a lot that I didn't know.

The problem with knowledge, or lack thereof, is that it can be hard to admit that you don't have all the answers all the time. The simple fact is that Nobody has all the answers. Ultimately, I chose the field of Mental Health, first as a nurse then as a Psychiatric Social Worker. I took advantage of the mentoring from a good Psychiatrist and a good Clinical Psychologist who were good enough to take me under their wings and teach me the survival skills necessary to be a good cognitive therapist.

But…if you asked me an in-depth question about labor and delivery of a baby or about the field of Neurology, I'd have to admit that I was well out of my league, and I'd refer the question to someone with expertise in that field. If I "bluffed" my way through an answer, I might have caused irreparable harm with a response that left the question unanswered or that led the questioner off in a direction that wouldn't help. Inflating your own ego to impress someone usually ends badly and your credibility suffers an unnecessary blow.

A b.s. artist usually enjoys only a brief stint in the limelight. Soon he is exposed as his information proves inaccurate and unreliable. Not knowing isn't a problem. Bluffing or being unwilling to learn however, IS.

CHAPTER 28

COMMUNICATION

Communication is one of the most important elements in our lives. It doesn't matter if you're 7 years old, 17, 37 or 70. It is a major part of our everyday existence, from the first "good morning" to the last "good night."

It comes in many forms, loud and soft, ordering or questioning, verbal and non-verbal. We communicate with body language, with our eyes and facial expressions, with hand gestures and with vocabulary. Each is used to transmit messages and feelings, and each inflection and word choice can change the thrust and the meaning in an active discussion. Be direct. Be decisive. Be a good listener. Communication works best when everybody is actively engaged in the process. Sometimes that ratio is 50 / 50, sometimes 80 / 20 or 20 / 80 (listening / talking) Communication can be used effectively or used to mislead the person listening or watching.

Everyone needs to be heard. A baby cries, letting his or her mother know that they are hungry or that they need to be changed. Like their older siblings who can communicate with words, they are sending a message with their cries. Verbal interaction changes in many ways as babies become bigger children, learning to talk and transmit their needs in other ways. A smile, a scowl, a blank stare, each sends a different message and alters communication.

It becomes more important as we mature, to say what you mean and mean what you say. The way we communicate changes. There are more options available to us. The verbal exchange between an infant and a mother evolves into the use of tools like the cell phone, X, Facebook, video chat and the list goes on and on. With the knowledge of each kind of communication tool, the responsibility to use it wisely and in a manner that doesn't violate rules and laws rests with us.

Some communication will seem dull and boring, like learning math or a subject in school that you really don't like. You'll hear the word "didactic" along the learning process. It's the book work that must be done before you can put knowledge into practical application. It can be dry or boring but is often the foundation upon which your future action is based.

Interpersonal communication takes on many forms. Here's where saying what you mean and meaning what you say begins to be more important. You'll hear the words "tell me the truth." It doesn't mean a version of the truth or a "half-truth" that you are trying to sell. It means the straightforward, unvarnished truth. You might employ the verbal trick of verbal sleight of hand, in which a little bit of your story is true but most of it, you are presenting to deceive the listener. The short-term gain from this trick seldom ends well. Trust after getting caught in this kind of exchange can be difficult to restore, so you're better off to say what you mean and mean what you say. Remember that. It's important.

Whether you're turning in a term paper or preparing for a debate in high school or applying online or being interviewed in person for a job or enlisting in the military or responding to questions by your girlfriend or wife or boss, your method of communication is important. Look the other person in the eye. It will tell you a lot about the person and will tell them a lot about you. Try not to monopolize the communication process in a discussion. Don't make it a speech unless asked to do so. You may well learn more by listening than by talking.

Communication ceases to be effective when it descends into an argument. Learning ceases and stubborn resistance comes to the surface, and all is lost. Enjoy the process of communication. Hone the skill. It will pay huge dividends to families, friends, education and jobs.

CHAPTER 29

DON'T BE AFRAID TO SAY "NO"

There will be times throughout your life when going with the flow or going along to get along well seem like the way to go. Don't be afraid to stop and think about your decisions. Is your decision to act based on instant gratification or is it a long-term solution to a nagging problem? Going along with your buddies or your girlfriends at the expense of someone else may carry with it repercussions or unanticipated consequences. Breaking the windows in the warehouse with rocks just the right size for throwing may sound like fun at the moment, but sitting in the police station waiting for your dad to come and take you home would put a damper on the excitement of the experience. When a friend threatens to end the friendship if you don't go along with his or her plan, saying NO is the better part of valor. Going along isn't being a friend. It's being used and almost never ends well. Staying in a relationship because you want to feel needed or want to rescue another person may sound and feel noble in the moment, but is more than likely a good time to back up, think about the dynamic and the end result, and say NO." When your friends want you to try illegal drugs or drinking when you're only 16, and you think that if you don't go along with it, they'll leave you, let them go. Think for yourself. It's OK to say, "no thanks" or "that doesn't sound like a good idea to me" or "I can't afford it" or "What are you, NUTS?" They aren't responsible for your decisions or your behavior. You Are.

Follow the Reasonable Man Theory. "If it sounds reasonable, all things considered, go for it. If it doesn't pass the smell test, walk away." The consequences are less, and the self-respect is greater. Sometimes Group Think is just the path of least resistance. Think for yourself and don't be afraid to say NO!

CHAPTER 30
YOU WON'T ALWAYS BE YOUNG

S ure, we all start out that way, little, cute, the apple of our mother's eye and all that stuff. You've probably already noticed changes as you careened through childhood. Preschool and Kindergarten were growing and learning experiences. Then you were "in the grades." That meant you were moving from being a little kid to being a big kid.

You were starting to make memories, but making your own decisions was still a little out of reach. Some of those memories will stay with you for the rest of your life: Your Kindergarten teacher, your first best friend and the first time you felt overwhelmed. Soon you're in double digits and you're 10. Now habits are forming, and your choices are beginning to be "your" choices, for better or for worse. You'll hear those words again further down the road. You're starting to notice bigger kids and their behavior choices. It will be called "peer pressure." It will start with little things like stealing candy from the convenience store or taking a dollar from your parents' dresser. Stealing is NOT OK, even if your friends do it. You'll see them bullying kids who don't quite fit in with the cool kids or can't defend themselves. You'll hear them brag about their exploits with their friends or anybody who might be willing to listen. You'll see other kids go along with them because they're afraid of the bully or because they wish they could get away with the behavior. You'll see kids sneaking beer or booze or pot, thinking that if they get away with it, they've "gotten away with it." They don't think about the damage they might have done or the consequences that might come if they get caught. Jails and prisons are full of inmates who thought they'd never get caught. That should be food for thought as you see the behaviors develop and can still resist the urge to be one of the cool kids. Bad behavior choices are never cool, EVER.

As you age, decisions take on a greater importance and carry greater consequences. Note: It might seem like we've spent a lot of time on Consequences. That's because they're a real thing and can be profoundly unpleasant. Look to your parents, your grandparents, aunts and uncles, a trusted teacher, your minister or your older brother or sister. If you have doubts about something, don't be afraid to ask for advice. They've probably faced the same or similar decision themselves. Treat them as a resource.

Soon you'll have to decide on the next phase of your life. High School will be in your rear-view mirror, and you'll be in the doorway of adulthood. Again, the decisions and the consequences will be greater. You'll encounter some of the same considerations that you made in years past, but their importance to your day-to-day life will have increased. Don't be afraid to look back on how you thought about that issue in the past and compare it to your thoughts today. You'll realize that you are growing and maturing. Embrace the change as a good thing. It's also inevitable.

There are now things to consider that are Matters of Consequence. You'll start to look into your future in a more mature way. Are you looking at college? Have you thought about the expense? Is trade school a better fit? Does military service interest you? If your dad or your grandfather served, ask them for their thoughts. It might be a family tradition. Here's where "Freedom Isn't Free" comes into play. Again, talk to someone you trust who will respond in your best interest. Talk to a military recruiter and learn the difference between Active Duty, Active Duty for Training, the National Guard, the Army, Navy or Air Force Reserve. Gather all the facts for each vocational option. Three years in the active military or 6 years in the Reserves may seem like a lifetime from the perspective on an 18-year-old but looking back with a sense of accomplishment and pride when you're in your 20's or 30's or 70's can make a difference in how you perceive yourself and how others perceive you.

There's something about being able to raise your hand when someone asks if there are any veterans in the crowd or when you stand and salute the flag or when the national anthem is played, knowing that you contributed to something greater than yourself and knowing that your contribution mattered to a lot of people besides you. Employers like to hire veterans and often will choose a vet, because of their maturity, their ability to problem solve and their ability to work effectively with people. It truly does matter.

I don't apologize for my obvious bias in writing this part of the book. I'm a proud Army veteran. My grandfather served in the Army in France in World War I. My dad's ship was in every major battle of the South Pacific in World War II. My brother Bill served three years in Viet Nam and three of my other brothers all served in either the Army, Navy or Air Force. My son followed both his mother and me into the Army Medical Corps and it's OK to be proud of that history. I can tell you from experience that it mattered in our lives and none of us would trade that experience for anything.

Your decisions will matter to you, to your family and to your friends, co-workers, employers and the list goes on and on. At some point you'll be looking toward retirement. All those decisions and their inherent success and failures that you made in your youth will become important again. Did you use your time wisely? Did you learn along the way? Did you correct your errors? It will all matter, so take yourself and your decisions seriously. When you think about it, you'll realize that every minute mattered and once gone into the history book, you can't get one minute back. Using each day as if it mattered, matters. So don't fritter your time away. Make each day count for something.

Enjoy the experience.

CHAPTER 31

BE CAREFUL WHO AND
WHAT YOU BELIEVE

Whether you're 6 or 60, it's important to listen carefully to what another person says and how it is said. Sometimes we are willingly gullible because we want to believe what we hear. It might be easier to follow a false statement because we either like or agree with the speaker. The older we get, the more careful we must become because in many cases, the stakes are higher.

When we were kids (there were 7 of us in our family) we had a kitchen culprit named "Nobody." When mom went to the cupboard to get the chocolate chips to make cookies and there were only 5 chips left in the bag, everyone of us said "I didn't do it." She finally decided that her 8th child must have taken them, and she put the blame on #8, "Nobody." It happened with marshmallows and raisin bread and the last piece of cake that she had saved for dad's lunch bucket. "Nobody" got around in our house, and we knew that mom knew. I still remember telling that lie, to this day, some 70 years later. "It wasn't me, mom."

It's not always about chocolate chips. As in many other things, as we get older, the stakes get higher. The lies get bigger, and the consequences paid increase. As a kid, when you came home full of mud and you told your mom that the kid down the block pushed you into the ditch, you upped the ante. Now you've dragged the neighbor kid into it, and he won't know what hit him when your mom calls his mom. It's a slippery slope that ends badly. It's called the "ripple effect." You have lied to your mother, lost a friend, his mother thinks less of you, and you're still covered with mud…and your dad isn't home from work YET. Do you get the picture?

Your mom believed you. The neighbor kid's mom believed him and nobody but you knows the truth...until your dad gets home.

Then there's the famous smoking incident when you were 10. Your mom asked if you were smoking. You said, "No, I wasn't smoking." You didn't know she had found the empty soup can in the garage with YOUR cigarette butts in it. You lied again and got caught red handed. Now your mom starts to think you are a liar and she stops trusting you. More consequences.

When your friend gives you the answers to the Algebra test, you fail because neither of you knew the questions on the final exam had been changed. You believed the liar who said he had the answers and now you have a failing grade. "But you said, those were the answers!!" "Sorry 'bout that." Was all he said...and you were out 10 bucks!

Like many other things, as you get older, the consequences get bigger. The adult world can be full of traps. Learn to sift through the information you are provided and providing and make your decisions with caution. There are always two sides to a story. It's important to know both sides. Back in Chapter 21, we talked about verbal sleight of hand and that which was left unsaid. These are traps, probably most used by politicians. The twist of context or leaving an important word or fact out of the conversation or story can completely change both the presentation and the response. The hero can come out looking like a scoundrel or a crook based on the merits of that which was said or that which was left unsaid. Support can be provided or withdrawn based on the truth or the lie.

The mainstream media can sway or even control an election by what it either broadcasts or refrains from broadcasting. In the 2020 Presidential election, the mainstream media refused to broadcast any positive news about the sitting President who was campaigning for re-election.

They broadcast only old, debunked stories that defamed him. They knew that the stories were untrue but along with our own FBI and social media, they were a part of the deception, and it worked. Social media blocked or censored users who disagreed with their corporate opinions or their manipulated political opinions and loyalties. This made it difficult or impossible to get a fair and balanced picture of either candidate. After months of only hearing their version of their narrative, the public to some extent became numb to the rhetoric or put off by their inability to get the whole picture. The media reflecting the images put forth by the Democrat party got pressured and or duped. Their focus became equality, racial equality, personal pronouns like he, she, they and them, critical race theory and the woke, cancel culture. They lost sight of national and international mismanagement, purposely hid verbal gaffs, illegal political maneuvering and a candidate who was obviously in a state of mental decline and challenge. The soon to be president had a long history of telling tall tales. The habit is difficult to recognize for some and difficult to break once it becomes common behavior. Verbal sleight of hand, that which was left unsaid and bald-faced lies become all too common and the faith that people once had in their elected government officials suffered what could be permanent damage.

So, beware of the little white lies that can set you on a negative course in the future and listen carefully to what people tell you. If in doubt, ask someone you trust or do your own research. It will pay large dividends down the road.

CHAPTER 32

IT'S NOT ALL ABOUT YOU

There's a growing trend in the youth of today. It's the feeling of "entitlement," where you think that somehow the world owes you something. To some degree, we've lost the concept of winners and losers. In real life "everybody" doesn't get a trophy just for participating. You shouldn't be "given" a passing grade just for perfect attendance. Not long ago, a college Organic Chemistry professor (who wrote the textbook in use) was terminated because a group of his students complained to the administration that his course was too hard. They felt entitled to a passing grade without earning it by sufficient effort. Organic Chemistry is known for its difficulty. Ask any medical student and they'll tell you.

To your parents, you are indeed special. To most of the world, not so much, unless you excel by your effort and accomplishment. It usually takes one to achieve the other. When you finish your education and enter the job market, you are usually one among many who may be applying for the same position. It can be humbling to realize that the world no longer revolves around you. You have competition for that job, and you may well fill out many applications before landing that perfect job. You might think that your newly acquired knowledge or degree in a given area is worth a bucket of money, but you may have to start at the lower-than-expected rate of pay and work your way up. Be secure in the knowledge that those who came before you to that company did not start in your dream job at 50K / year.

Many graduates can't find work in their chosen field of study. Again, you aren't special. You are one of many. A degree in Philosophy might not be the right degree to land that perfect job. In many fields, it is more about the people with whom you have come in contact than it is just about you.

Teachers, nurses, fire fighters, doctors and police officers all choose to serve the public. Being important is not usually their primary motivation in job choice. Being effective and doing something that matters, probably is. The student who looks up to a teacher and wants to become a teacher him or herself, learns by and is motivated by the example of that teacher.

In some cases, you or your acquired skills may indeed be special. The talented boxer or baseball player, quarterback or movie star can gain fame and fortune and start thinking that it is indeed all about them, but without careful consideration of the sometimes-short lived fame, they may end up poor and wondering "what happened here?" They got to feel important. They got (and paid for) highly paid managers, trainers, drivers and dinner dates. They spent their money as fast as they made it or worse, spent it in anticipation of what was surely to come. Then the football star breaks his leg and his career is over. His manager squanders the star's money, and they all end up broke. Riding high only lasts just so long for most. Then the harsh reality hits and they must make a living like everybody else, and it can be a bitter pill to swallow. If you still think it's all about you...rethink that.

CHAPTER 33

IT'S ALL ABOUT SPIT.......JUST SAYIN'

Yes, Really! Some people spit in order to look tough or to intimidate another person. Chewing Tobacco or snuff users spit into Styrofoam cups, not caring that it looks disgusting to the non-chewers or snuffers.

But...a lick or two of spit on your fingers and rubbed on a mosquito or chigger or horse fly or fire ant bite and the worst itching that you've probably ever experienced will be significantly reduced or will disappear entirely.

No Kidding!

CHAPTER 34

WANT VS. NEED

One is often not related to the other. Some will call it "The Wants." They can range from a candy bar to a candy apple red car, but it is absolutely natural to want things. A kid wants a new bike or a new computer game. A twenty-something wants a new job. Parents want to give their kids opportunities to learn or maybe a birthday present that they don't expect. Newly marrieds want to buy a house or start a family. Long-term employees want to retire with enough money to be comfortable. The list is endless and depends largely on your age and financial station in life.

Your wants may not coincide with your resources. Therein lies the rub. By necessity, your needs may well take priority over your wants and your ability to support your wants financially (or not) may be a determining factor. The same candy bar that cost 10 cents in 1958 may not be in your budget in 2025 when it now costs $2.25. The candy apple red car may be nothing more than a fantasy or a pipe dream when you're 23 and starting your first real job. When you're a teenager, you might have to babysit or deliver papers or mow yards or bag groceries to afford that new mountain bike or cell phone or video game. Now we're back to the concept of earn-to-have which is directly related to Want vs. Need.

As time has passed, the way kids earn their spending money has changed. Many of us who grew up in the 1950's and 60's, really did mow yards for 50 Cents or a dollar or babysit for $2.00 on New Year's Eve (not $2.00 / Hour, $2.00 for the evening.) The kids of today, in the 2020's would probably laugh at offerings like that and say, "I'm Not Going To Do THAT!" but we recognize that times and prices and methods of earning have changed significantly. The genuine needs probably haven't changed all that much, but the concept of wanting may well be much greater than in the past as quantity and opportunity have evolved.

The parents of the 1950's and 60's did a lot of going without so their kids could have a better go of it than they had as children in the 1930's. Parents of today still go without so their kids can have some of those opportunities that were missed in previous generations. Going to private school or helping pay for college are still expensive, even more so than in years past. You may not recognize their sacrifice but rest assured, it is probably there, right under your nose. It's what parents are inclined by their nature to do.

After a long career, an employee will need to have saved enough money during his or her working life to pay the mortgage, rent or light bill or the car payment or health insurance when they are no longer in the active work force. That financial stability is a need based on a want. The candy bar, the car, the new computer or vacation are not needed in most cases. They are wants. Sometimes you can go from want to need seamlessly. At other times, the wants need to be re-considered.

One method in addressing wants is to wait two weeks, time used to measure the real need and the related ability to justify a purchase or investment. Everybody has wants, both those that are fleeting and quickly forgotten and those that may nag at you and are based in the category of need. It can often be a series of events, need / want or want / need, followed quickly by earn / have.

There are variables that affect the concepts of want and need. Family circumstances differ. Social position, geography, number of siblings and relation to resources and careers, all contribute to the phenomenon of want vs. need. Those are considerations that haven't changed much as time marches on. Pay attention. Be patient and think before you act.

CHAPTER 35

DON'T OVERTHINK IT

Everybody faces problems and challenges, large and small. What begins as a challenge can become a real problem. Much can depend on the manner you employ to reach a resolution that is acceptable to you and the situation at hand.

There are people who think deliberately from one basic step to another. There are people who act spontaneously with little calculation or thought, and there are those who ruminate on an issue or situation, running it over and over in their minds until they get mired down in confused details, some of which are not at all relevant to the solution. They feel pressured to solve the problem RIGHT NOW, but are so confused by extraneous, irrelevant details that right now never happens. They become paralyzed and unable to think clearly, leading to anxiety or depression. Pressured thoughts and feelings spin around in your mind. The thread of thoughts that lead to solutions gets lost and your mind basically shuts down or spins out of control.

This is the time to seek out someone you trust to help you regain your perspective and your control. That someone becomes a resource and may be able to slow you down enough to regain control of the situation yourself. Obsessive thoughts and ruminating seldom lead to resolution. Take the elements of the issue one at a time, from the most important to the least. Identify your options and list them from the most likely to succeed. This will allow you to respond with a logical conclusion instead of reacting to a barrage of complicated, immobilizing possibilities.

CHAPTER 36

WORK SMARTER, NOT HARDER

You may hear this more than once, especially if you work on projects that include concerted physical effort. You'll hear "lift with your legs, not your back." This won't make an impression until you pull the muscles in your lower back while lifting the end of the couch when you're moving into a new apartment or leaning deep into the trunk of your car at an awkward angle with a box of books.

If you're a tool, project repair kind of person, think before you pick up pliers where a box wrench is in order. You'll remember this the first time the pliers slip, and you take the skin off your knuckles. When the warning on the 3rd step from the top on the ladder says "don't climb or stand above this step" take heed. A fall from a ladder hurts, sometimes for a long time. Buy a 4 ft. ladder and an 8 ft. ladder for your house or garage.

There's also an academic application for this bit of wisdom. Outline before you write that essay. Make a story board before you write a children's book. Line your ducks up before you start a writing project. Have someone else proofread your books, term papers or research papers. Reread your own work before you give it to the proofreader. Spend as much time researching as you do writing. It may seem like a lot of steps, but it is the shortest way to complete a project. (Research, Outline Adjust Outline, Write draft, Reread, Adjust draft, and proof for content, grammar and punctuation. Finish draft, have it typed and proofed, then submit your work)

And…if you wake up at 2 AM with a eureka moment of an idea, get up. Write it down in as much detail as you can. Then go back to sleep. If you don't follow this rule, you will have forgotten the idea and the details by morning.

You'll either forget it completely or you'll only remember disconnected fragments of the thought and the moment, and the idea will be lost. Remember, your subconscious works even when you are asleep.

Think about your project before diving into it feet first. Have a Plan "A" and oftentimes have a Plan "B". When you're making dinner for guests, make a list and, like Santa Clause, look at it twice. See what you already have on hand and only make one trip to the store. That way you won't end up with 3 jars of pickles and no cinnamon and you won't be scrambling when the doorbell rings and your guests arrive.

Forethought and planning are always preferable to hindsight and disappointment. The latter can leave you frustrated. Pace yourself, prioritize, take a break and enjoy the satisfaction of a job well done.

CHAPTER 37

SEIZE THE DAY

There's more to this bit of wisdom than a song from the movie "Newsies. "It can be applied to most people on most days throughout their lives. A lot of people coast through life, with little recognition of the opportunities and challenges that do everything but hit them in the face in order to be noticed. It's easy to coast, to say "I'll do it later" or "Let somebody else do it." It can be harder to take up the challenge and say, "I'd like to try that" or I'll take care of that.

There are benefits to taking on the challenge, to seizing the day. When the end of the day comes and you take stock of your contribution and accomplishments for yourself or for what is called "" the greater good," you are left with your contribution and either satisfaction or disappointment. It's all up to you and it doesn't matter if you're 14 or 81. Accomplishing something that matters, matters. The kid who volunteers to clean up after the school play or your brother who helps you paint your room or the old man who picks up trash along the lake shore in the state forest, each makes a difference in their own lives and in the lives of others.

Sometimes it's a public display of citizenship. You help and are noticed and rewarded for your effort. There's nothing wrong with that. You put effort into it, and you get something back in return. You have an accomplishment and an ego boost, all at the same time. Sometimes nobody sees and your contribution goes unnoticed by anyone until long afterwards. You get self-satisfaction from the effort, knowing that you could have just as easily let someone else do it, but you didn't.

There's a group of volunteers in the state forest, four couples who are winter season campground hosts and two of us who are year-round general volunteers

They're all in their 60's and 70's, old by most standards to still be working. They pick up trash, clean bathrooms and fire pits, repair buildings, equipment and roads and almost nobody knows their names. One of the campers asked one of the volunteers on day, "You do this for nothing?" The volunteer looked around the beautifully maintained campground, full of tents, campers, motor homes, bikes, skateboards, canoes, kayaks and kids, looked at the young man with the question and quietly said, "I'm 75 years old, retired and healthy and I get to work outside every day, in a beautiful forest with people that are a lot like me, doing something that we like to do and we still get to do something that matters." My hope is that you too, someday have that opportunity.

Seizing the day has no age restriction, no academic or occupational boundaries. It is an individual choice and is always better than the alternative.

CHAPTER 38

TAKE NOBODY AND NOTHING FOR GRANTED

The operative term is "For Granted." Don't assume that somebody is going to do something just because he's a nice guy or she's a nice lady. Situations change and people tend to change their behavior with altered circumstances or in some cases with the change in the direction of the wind

By the same token, don't automatically assume the worst from someone because somebody else said something bad or negative about them. Be your own person and trust your own observation and judgement...But be sure you have all the necessary information before you commit time, energy or money based on an assumption. You'll learn the term Due Diligence along your journey. It's more than just a cautionary term.

Here's where intellect and emotion can prove to be bitter enemies. Always...Always base your decisions on intellect. The logical thought process of identifying the pros and cons of an issue or question is intellectual, not in a nerdy way but in a reasonable way. It must make sense, like 2+2 must equal 4. When a decision is based on emotion, logic is pushed aside, and you decide that way because you wanted it that way or you assumed that you could trust someone's judgement without knowing the necessary information. That's what's known as faulty reasoning, and you'll pay an unanticipated price for your not so well thought out trust.

This leads us to The Reasonable Man Theory. The saying goes, "If it sounds too good to be true, it's probably too good to be true." At every age imaginable, from your teens to your 80's, you'll have people approach you with "the best deal you've ever seen," on any number of goods from steak knives to cars to guns and marketing schemes. Some will sound wonderful (unbelievable), full of promise and instant, huge rewards.

Don't believe it for a minute. Remember, if it's too good to be true, etc. You'll see rockets and shooting stars and shortly after you've made the deal of the day and parted with your hard-earned money, you'll figure out that the person who promised you the moon, was full of hot air. His scam has worked and he's nowhere to be found. He's in the wind and you're standing there with a car full of bodywork and an engine that sputters and coughs. You've bought the answers to the upcoming algebra test, and you still got an "F" because the teacher made up a new test. You'll feel embarrassed and angry and there's nothing you can do to fix your mistaken trust except to learn from it. Use the adage, "Buyer Beware." It will save you a lot of money, frustration and heartache.

Know the people you are dealing with, personally or from reliable, verified information. Pie-in-the-sky deals need to be balanced by reasonable expectations, sometimes exhaustive research, and at times a "thanks but no thanks. I'll pass on this one." It's called the Reasonable Man Theory for a reason. At the onset, some super deals won't pass the sniff test. You'll get the feeling that there's just something wrong with the deal. You can't put your finger on it, but it just doesn't feel right. Here is where you follow your intellect and reason and, in most cases, you'll be right.

The theory also works on Want vs. Need. My dad used to say "Wait two weeks: when I'd tell him I wanted something Really Badly. In my young life and newfound earned income, there were a lot of times when saving my money for something that I both wanted and needed worked out better in two weeks and sure enough, my want had evolved into another quest. I didn't need the new ball glove or the new computer app. (my age vs. your age). My grandfather told me to take half of whatever I got paid from my part-time jobs and put it in the bank and to enjoy what was left. It was good advice. It was reasonable and it has worked often. The grass is not always greener, and the deal is not always, no matter how good it sounds.

CHAPTER 39

HE SAID. SHE SAID.
IF IT'S NOT IN WRITING

The bottom line is, in many cases, if it's not in writing, it didn't happen. Somewhere along the way, you'll be in a situation where you must verify that something either happened or didn't happen. Don't be fooled by somebody saying something of consequence that you may not have seen or heard yourself. It's called Hearsay.

In business, in law enforcement, in the military, in any kind of investigation, if it is not in writing or on film, it can't be proved and will not stand up in court. Listen for proof and look for evidence. A good example is in the case of an insurance investigation of a car accident. Without a police report, it's your word against the other person involved and the insurance company won't want to pay for the damage if it was your fault. This is especially true in the case of severe bodily injury, ambulance rides, hospital and ER stays, doctor visits after the accident etc. etc. The out-of-pocket costs can amount to many thousands of dollars, and somebody must pay the bill. An accident left unreported because you were trying to hide an infraction or protect your own driving record could lead to a lawsuit by a perceived victim, acting out of hostilities between those involved along with stress and anxiety that last long after the accident. No-fault insurance is not yet a national mandate and you could be held liable. You could tell the insurance agent "he said or did blah, blah, blah...when in fact it isn't true. Always back up your story or your position with written, verified or picture proof. It will save you a lot of frustration, grief and potentially a lot of money. When the ambiguous "they" did or said something, it means nothing. Get the proof.

CHAPTER 40

TALK "TO" PEOPLE. NOT "AT" THEM

Listen carefully to verbal communication, whether it's in a large group in a lecture hall or a church service, whether it's in a small interactive group or a conversation with one other person. Watch the speakers' eyes and body language when you are being spoken to. Particularly in small groups or a one-on-one setting, you will be able to tell a lot about the speaker and his or her message by the quality of the eye contact between you. When you respond verbally that person will also be able to measure the level of interest and attention that you return to him or her. The speaker will be watching you, too.

If a speaker spends most of his or her energy reading from a prepared script, the amount of direct eye contact is limited and at least some of the audience will lose interest in the presentation. The ability to command and sustain the interest of the audience, be it large or small, depends on the subject matter, the composition of the audience and manner of presentation.

Make eye contact. Speak at a level and in a manner that will ensure their interest and understanding. Let the audience, whether large or small, know that you want to be there, that you are interested in the subject at hand and that their interest and involvement matters to you.

CHAPTER 41

DON'T MAKE THE SAME MISTAKE TWICE

Be aware that everyone, man, woman and child, makes mistakes. Some are small and easily glossed over and corrected. Others are bone-headed gaffes that require apologies, accountability and compensation. Most of us will make each of these during our lives. Reconcile yourself to that fact. It's a natural part of life. We're all human.

What separates the men from the boys is our ability to overcome the embarrassment and the consequences and learn enough from the mistake to not repeat it. Though probably overgeneralized, I was told by my dad that I was allowed to make one mistake every day but not to make the same mistake twice. Though not the most eloquent man on earth, he was very wise, and he and my mother raised seven children to adulthood, teaching by example, and it worked. Three of us ended up in prison. (We worked there. We didn't live there.) We all made mistakes, both large and small.

Some folks can admit their errors, learn from them and move on. Others, whether guided by greed, stupidity or lack of conscience, repeat the act for ill-gotten gain and pay a far greater price. Loss of reputation doesn't matter to them. The risk of getting caught is outweighed by the thrill attached to the act, the perceived reward or the perceived need for the adrenaline rush of the risk.

One of my patients in the prison Mental Health Dept. called it "thrills for skills" and when I asked him how many years he was doing, he said, "I'm only doing a quick nickel." That's five years and it didn't matter one whit to him.

The thief who breaks into cars or houses to steal valuables to sell, repeats the same mistake over and over, thinking or not even considering the thought of getting caught.

Even after a couple years in prison, the urge to profit quickly from a risk often overcomes the recent memory of the prison cell, the danger, the time lost and the associated losses because of his or her actions. Sometimes it's called amoral or an anti-social personality disorder or desperation (in the case of a drug addict). Often the repeater denies or ignores the rules of society, placing his or her needs and wants above all else. The pathological liar loses sight of the truth and or his ability to discern right from wrong or truth from fiction.

One lie requires another and another to cover the first. After a while, the lie is just as natural to them as the truth is for normal people. It's still a mistake and still requires addressing at some point. In some cases that point never comes. Accountability passes by and the lesson goes unlearned. That, too, is the reality for some. If they notice at all, it is an incidental event in life and the mistake becomes their lifestyle.

CHAPTER 42

CHOICES

There's an old Clint Eastwood Movie called The Good, The Bad and the Ugly. We all face choices in our daily lives. Choosing wisely can be a challenge. At times a lot of our choices involve people, including ourselves, and events, one often dependent on the other. We can choose wisely, rendering a positive result or we can make a poor choice with disastrous results.

Joining the Army or Navy can fall under the first category, giving us valuable knowledge and training, travel and unmatched experience. Joining a gang on the other hand can bring excitement, danger, physical harm to yourself or someone else and the risk of arrest and jail time, hence the terms, The Good and the Bad. The Ugly comes next and is a result of the bad choices. Choosing to do damage to others, whether physical or emotional, is the ugly side of the choice. There is no redeeming quality to this choice and no tangible positive outcome. The choice carries with it consequences, sometimes harsh and far reaching, sometimes never ending.

Think first and then choose wisely.

CHAPTER 43

THE TUG – O - WAR

The saying goes, "You can't have a Tug - O- War with no one at the other end of the rope." A phrase, more true was never written.

Interpersonal relationships are complicated. They don't have to be difficult, but under the right circumstances, they certainly can be. The end result of a disagreement between two people who are unwilling or unable to agree or reach a compromise can be the dissolution of a friendship or a breakdown in the discussion of the subject at hand. Their individual inability to sway the other's point of view has led to a counterproductive back and forth where the goal becomes to inflict some damage without it appearing that that goal is the intent.

It's sometimes difficult to determine which comes first or is first used as a weapon, aggression or passive aggressive attacks that may or may not be related to the basic issue at hand. Each party is pulling as hard as they can on the rope with neither gaining nor losing ground. Each resort to attacking the other's perspective by attacking or casting aspersions on his character, which may or may not have anything to do with the issue at hand. The relationship has become adversarial, and neither is likely to achieve the desired outcome. The tugging continues on both sides with no winner in sight. Arguments become heated. Things are said that you may regret later or that inflict long-lasting harm to an otherwise reasonable relationship. "Cheap shots" are exchanged, leaving one or both parties feeling vulnerable to the other, but neither is willing to give an inch or let go of the proverbial rope.

There is, however, a tactic that can minimize the potential damage to a fragile ego on the other side or prevent you from saying something that you will surely regret later. Let Go of The Damn Rope!! Leave the aggressor with his own words ringing in his own ears, not yours. Let the situation calm down, giving all concerned time to think before re-engaging in the exchange of thoughts, feelings and ideas.

In most disagreements of this nature, time is usually not a critical element and resolution may well be attainable after one or both verbal combatants have had the opportunity to re-evaluate his or her position and the reality of the end result seeps into the exchange.

In most cases, letting go of the rope doesn't mean that you give up or abdicate your position. It simply means that you make a conscious choice to allow time to temper the situation and perhaps change the perspective for when the bell rings and you both pick up your respective ends of the rope.

CHAPTER 44
WHAT YOU DO VS. WHO YOU ARE

Yes, there's more than a semantic difference between the two. What you do involves action on your part. It involves movement and response to a stimulus or to the behavior of somebody else. In baseball, a runner is thrown out at first base as a direct result of a pitcher hurling a fastball at 97 miles an hour and a batter running to first base after breaking his bat on a ground ball to the shortstop. It is sometimes called a mechanical response, a response to a stimulus. It has little or nothing to do with who the person is. My dad was a butcher at Oscar Mayer & Co. He boned pork shoulders in a 38-degree room called "The Cut Floor" for more than 30 years with the same group of maybe a dozen other men, most of whom had fought in World War II. They put meat in grocery stores and in meat market cases for doctors and lawyers, ministers and miners to buy for their family's supper tables. It was "what they did" and had very little to do with who they were.

Now let's look at Who They Were. The operative is now, "Who". The pitcher in the first paragraph was the leader of his team. The other players looked up to him with respect because they knew he was honest, hardworking, moral and could encourage the other players to do their best. The shortstop was a grandfather, maybe a little old to still be playing that position but he had dedication to the game and to his teammates. He was loyal and could hit like a 25 yr. old. The batter was a kid in comparison, 18 yrs. Old, loud selfish, stubborn and didn't care what anybody thought of him. That, in a nutshell was Who he was. When he was called OUT! At first base, he swore loud enough that the kids in the 5th row of bleachers could hear him. That is both what he did and who he was.

Let's go back to the butcher for a quick minute. He wasn't just a butcher. He was a dad to seven kids, a husband and an usher at church. He spent time with his children, fishing, hiking and playing catch, watching them grow through childhood, using him as an example of how to live life in the best way he knew how. Quietly, he shed a tear each time he took one of his sons to the train station on their way to Basic Training in the military; two to the Army, two to the Navy and one to the Air Force. Dad knew that freedom isn't free and with each son's departure, he was sad, worried and proud, all at the same time. That's the measure of Who a person is. What you do is behavior and recognizable as that. Who you are is a measure of your character and is just as recognizable. Others notice both, sometimes individually and sometimes both at the same time. Be aware of how one reflects on the other as you travel on your journey through life.

CHAPTER 45

DON'T BE AFRAID TO SAY IT

There are times in each of our lives when "Something" needs to be said. Sometimes it's to correct incorrect or missing information. Sometimes it's necessary to change the direction of a conversation or situation. Sometimes it's to inject just a little bit of levity into a strained circumstance and sometimes you just can't help yourself and you blurt something out that you think a recipient just can't do without. There are also times when saying Nothing is the best plan or the better part of valor.

Saying what you mean at the right time is a vital element in any relationship, whether it's between you and your mom or dad, you and your girlfriend or boyfriend, your husband, wife or your boss. Each situation needs to be considered on its own merit and the risk involved in bringing up a potentially touchy subject, or the risk in provoking a negative response.

In the risk / reward scenario, there are times when someone desperately needs to hear what you have to say or just needs a word of encouragement or recognition. Acknowledging the effort that a person has put into a relationship or circumstance can mean the world to a person who feels alone, left out or unappreciated. A simple "I love you" or "I appreciate what you tried to do" or "It's always good to see you" can go a long way toward a better day. The older we get, the more important that simple acknowledgement of another person becomes. A very wise person once said, "Don't come to mourn at my grave after I'm gone. I'm not there anymore. Come and have coffee with me while I'm alive and can enjoy our conversation.

SANDBOX 101
FINAL NOTE

There's a literary process in which a person writes primarily from his or her own experiences. This book is an example of that process. The narratives that make up each chapter are from the author's own life experience, an amalgam of thoughts and feelings that grew from the seeds planted by family, old friends and old volunteers who gather each morning for coffee on the workbench in the state forest wood shop in Florida. The shared collective wisdom is our gift to readers of any age.

The chorus of an old Kingston Trio song called Desert Pete seems like a good way to end this journey. The setting is an old well in what seems to be a hot, dry desolate stretch of uninhabitable desert. The only visible sign of hope is a clear mason jar on the edge of a weathered old well. You, the reader, are the traveler in need of water.

The lesson goes like this: "You've got to prime the pump. You must have faith and believe. You've got to give of yourself before you're worthy to receive. Drink all the water you can hold. Wash your face. Cool your feet but leave a bottle full for others. Thank you kindly, Desert Pete."

There are a lot of lessons in the words of the song and the pages of this book. Some will laugh at the lessons, and some will ignore them entirely. Some will realize that a lesson or two will apply intimately to them or someone they know. If you choose to take a lesson or two to heart, it may take a bump or two out of the road. That's the goal of this book. I hope you enjoyed the journey that began in the sandbox on Hargrove Street when I was four and will continue for the rest of our lives.

My Best To You,   Jerome B. Imhoff

Printed in the United States
by Baker & Taylor Publisher Services